FILM FOR HER

DARSHIKA SHARMA

BookLeaf Publishing

India | USA | UK

Presentation by *BookLeaf Publishing*

Web: www.bookleafpub.com
E-mail: info@bookleafpub.com

ISBN: 9789369537341

First edition 2025

To the ones who bloom gently, where no one thought to look.
You are never a moment; you're an experience
:) Much love to mom & dad

Contents

Acknowledgments

With ink-stained hands and a heart full of reverence, I offer my deepest gratitude to those who stood beside me as Film for Her took form.

To my dearest family—your quiet faith has been my compass, guiding me through every uncertain word. To my teachers—your wisdom has been the soil in which my thoughts have grown, steady and wild. And to the publishing team— thank you for honoring the fragile world I've built with such care and clarity.

To every reader who breathes life into these pages—thank you. Your presence completes this work.

This is only the first bloom of many. Stories still stir within me—unfinished, unnamed—but they are coming.

With grace and ink, Darshika

Preface

This was never meant to be a book.

It began as a quiet place where I could feel without flinching— a space for the things I never said out loud, the feelings that didn't ask to be understood, only written.

Film for Her is not about a person, but about what it means to be human—to long, to lose, to remember, and to keep loving the world even when it doesn't love you back.

These poems are pieces of time I couldn't let go. A collection of pauses, glances, and moments that lived longer in my mind than they did in reality. They are what remain when life moves on but your heart stays behind.

In these pages, I tried to capture the stillness between heartbeats, the kind of quiet that only poetry understands— and I offer it now to you.

If you find something of yourself here, something you once felt but could never explain, then maybe this book was always yours too.

Because poetry isn't about answers. It's about remembering that we still feel. That we're still alive.

—DARSHIKA

Distant Echoes

I knew you in ways the world could not—
Not through the heavy breath of passing time,
But in the quiet spaces between words,
In the moments our silence spoke louder than our voices.

I knew your laughter as one knows the comfort of morning light—
Unrushed, pure, casting shadows in its wake.
Now, I search for it in the hollow corners
Of rooms where you no longer walk,
Where the air is still, thick with memories.

I knew the rhythm of your hands,
Their touch, their reach, their purpose.
Now, they linger only in the phantom pulse of my own,
And I wonder if you ever knew how much you left behind.

You were once the echo of my heart's beat,
But time, cruel as it is, distorts what was certain.
Now, all I have are these fading thoughts,
And a distance that never truly closes.

Too Close to Be Far

i see you.
not in the way i used to,
not in the way i'd like to

present, but not near
a glance. a silence.
a space that was never there before.

they say distance is measured in miles.
but i have never been farther from you than the time
when you stood right next to me.

i want to call out your name—
but names feel like spells,
and i am afraid of what will break
if i speak.

so i let the silence hold us.
let the air between us stretch,
tight as a rope, thin as regret.

you are here. i am here.
but we are nowhere at all.

The Garden That Withered

I was the garden you once tended,
Every seed of mine to you, I surrendered.
With roots entwined in tender care,
I gave you flowers, unaware.

You walked through me, a careless breeze,
Trampling petals, breaking leaves with ease.
Each step you took was a heavy rain,
Drowning the bloom, feeding the pain.

I gave you the sun, and still you fled,
With every step, the petals bled.
And though I wept, I couldn't resist—
Loving you was the only truth I missed.

You built your path upon my soul,
A trail of dust where love once was whole.
Yet, as you walked away, I remained—
A garden that withers but still sustained.

Untold

I'm not who I was yesterday—
The mirror shows someone different
But deep inside, beneath it all,
There's a part of me you never understood.

The world keeps moving, keeps dragging me along,
I'm learning to laugh, therefore pretending I'm strong.
But there are thorns of whispers I can't let go,
Stories I hide, feelings I don't dare to show.

It's not that I don't want to speak,
It's just... some things feel way too weak.
So I feel safe to keep them locked.

I smile at change; let the current take me,
But these shadows inside won't set me free.
They cling to my chest; they echo and fold—
These are the feelings I've never told.

Would you ever understand if I let you in?
Or would my hidden truth feel like a sin?

Almost Strangers

i see you,
but i don't say hi.
you see me,
but you don't try.

we used to talk till 2 a.m.,
laugh till our stomachs hurt.
now it's just passing
pretending it doesn't still burn.

i hear your name in someone's mouth,
and it still hits the same.
like a song i used to love,
but now i skip the refrain.

we didn't fight; we didn't break,
no slammed doors, no last mistake.
just time, just space,
just something we can't erase.

we're not enemies; we're not friends,
just a story that won't extend.
too close to be nothing,
too far to be again.

Framed By Life

You told me it was the wrong timing,
That we were born too early or far too late.
But I don't believe that's the truth—
It's just the way life frames itself,
The way our hearts are torn between fate and the unknown.

The right person, they say, will come when it's meant to be,
But what if timing is never on our side?
What if the world is only ever a few breaths too late?
We built a house together, you and I—
But we had no tools to keep it standing.

I gave you my heart, brick by brick,
But love needs more than just hope to stick.
We were the walls, the foundation, the dream,
But without the right hands, it all crumbled at the seams.

We wanted forever, thought we could hold on—
But time slipped through like sand in a storm.
We had the love; we had the vision,
But life wasn't kind enough to give us the conditions.

Right person, wrong timing, they say—
But that's no excuse, is it?
Maybe life doesn't care about our timing,
It just builds us up, breaks us down,
And asks us to keep going, even when we're left with nothing
but dust.

What Are We?

I wonder if you ever look at me
the way I still look at you.
Like a memory half-forgotten,
but never really gone.

I wonder if you ever hear my name
and feel something shift inside—
not pain, not longing,
just the ghost of something that was once alive.

I wonder if we're both waiting
for the other to say something first.
Or if we've already said everything
in the silence.
Almost, Always

There's a song playing somewhere,
one we used to sing too loud,
off-key,
like we didn't care who heard.
Now, I turn the volume down.

We are not strangers,
but we are not us.

Not Quite

I am the echo of applause,
the almost-bright star
beside the sun.
Good, they say,
but not the one they'd like to cheer for.

I stood as the second choice,
the one who tries just enough
to matter,
but not enough to stay.

The weight of "not best"
is heavy in my chest.
It curls in the corners of my mind,
whispering things what I already know—
That close is not enough.

I watch others rise,
their names carved in moments
I'll never own.
My hands tend to reach
but always fall short.

And when they look at me,
it's with soft eyes that don't linger.
Good, but forgettable.
A space filled by anyone else.

Fading

I want to dissolve into the quiet mist,
become the air between our breaths,
the pause after a thought.

To shed this weight of self—
this face, this name,
the endless need to mean something special.

It feels simple, doesn't it?
To step off the edge of knowing,
to sink into nothing,
Or be forgotten
even by myself

No more mirrors,
no more voices calling me to stay
just the hum of absence,
and the ease of being lost.

But somewhere beneath the wanting,
a whisper stirs me deep
It asks,
who am I without this weight?
And why do I still hold on?

But Gone Before I Can Hold You

In your storm, I find my pain,
Yet without you, I'm not the same.
For your thunder cracks my silent shell,
A storm within that I
can't quell.

You are the tempest that rattles my peace,
The spark that fuels my wild release.
But like the lightning, you disappear—
Leaving nothing but silence and the weight of fear.

Yet, I am drawn to you, the storm, the flame,
For in your fury, I find my name.
Thunder and lightning, chaos and calm,
In your storm, I find my balm.
But gone before I can hold you.

Yet, I am drawn to you, the storm, the flame,
For in your fury, I find my name.
Thunder and lightning, chaos and calm,
In your storm, I find my balm.

Unseen, Yet Known

No mirror can capture the way I have become,
For beauty is the quiet trust in one's own heart,
The soft hum of being seen,
Not by eyes, but by the depth of a knowing touch.

I find it in the way the world bends toward me,
Not in grand gestures, but in stillness,
In the grace of breathing in a world that spins
Without asking if I'm ready.

The beauty lies in the strength I hold in silence—
In the way I rise, not because I am told,
But because the fire within me refuses to be quenched.
I am not seen through glass, but through the soul's own gaze.

I am the quiet force that moves mountains without sound,
The grace that leaves its mark, unspoken,
And when the world wonders if I am enough,
I smile, for I know the answer lies within.

Unfinished Art

Love spills like ink on trembling skin,
a masterpiece that's lost before it tends to begin.
Colors ache, shadows yearn,
brushstrokes whisper; hub still burns.

Fingers trace what has no chance to stay
fading light in sculpted clay.
A soul is captured, never held,
a love that's untold, a story spelled.

Yet canvas waits with quiet grace,
for one more stroke, one last embrace.
etched in longing, bound by pain.

Red

You quietly loved me—
like a song half-played on vinyl crackle,
like lipstick stains on whiskey glass,
like prayers whispered in motel chapels.

The summer burned in golden blues,
your hands like ghosts along my spine.
We kissed beneath the neon lights,
drunk on love and borrowed time.

But darling, love was never kind,
not to girls who dream in black and white.
I traced your name in cigarette smoke,
but you were gone before the night.

So here I sit, in cherry red,
a fragile thing, a heart undone.
Loving you was lace and leather—
Soft... reckless

Ist Choice

I'm good at everything, but never quite enough to shine
A person who never wins the applause
A singer with no stage to call mine
Like a quiet star in a crowded sky
Always glowing, never blazing
People, they clap for the winners,
They cry for the broken,
But what about the one in between?
The one who tries just enough
The one ehos just pretty good
I ace the tests, but no one remembers my name
It's their cheers that echo
Not mine
The backup plan—always there but never 1st choice
They call me talented, but their words feel hollow
Like applause in an empty room
Maybe being good at everything means
Being great at nothing
So I carry this curse
A weight I can't put down
Of being everything to everybody
But nothing that lingers
Good enough to be noticed
Never enough to be remembered.

Some People Walk Like A Sin, And I Pray To Them

Some people don't just walk into a room—they arrive.
Like the slow burn of a match kissed to gasoline,
like the first inhale of a cigarette you swore you'd quit.

They wear arrogance like silk,
grace like something they were born drowning in.
The kind of beauty that isn't asked for,
but demanded—not in shouts, but in the hush that follows.

Their gaze?
Sharp enough to carve scripture into skin.
Their mouth?
A crime scene of words never meant to be spoken.
They could say your name once
and have it feel like a prophecy.

They don't rush.
The world moves around them,
adjusts, accommodates, aches.
Because some people don't just exist—
they are something to be witnessed.

And if you're lucky,
just once,
they might look at you
like you're worth remembering.

Warmth I Never Owned

She wore silence like a second skin
A warmth I could never hold—
Not for the lack of trying
But because she belonged to the world
And I just kept watching
Her hair smelled like belonging not to me
I counted seconds between her glances
As if they were prayers—
Unanswered but still holy
She touched my arm and the sky opened
I stood in the rain

A Love That Took Me

I loved you like the tide loves shore,
Rushing in, then begging more.
I gave you all, my breath, my name,
Until I was a ghost in frame.

I traced my soul along your spine,
Let yours consume the whole of mine.
A quiet death, a velvet ache,
A love that gave, a love that takes.

I was the moon; you were the sea,
You pulled, I drowned so willingly.
And in the waves, I slipped away—
A shadow lost in endless gray.

Now who am I? What have I left?
A name once whispered, now bereft.
For loving you, I paid my due,
And lost the girl you never knew.

Hold Me Like A Quiet Poem

Hold me like a whisper,
like a secret the night keeps.
Soft hands, slow breaths,
a love so quiet
it hums between heartbeats.

Trace constellations on my skin,
name the freckles,
call them yours.
Let time melt between our fingers,
let the world exist somewhere far, far away.

No grand confessions,
no burning need—
just this, just us,
wrapped in the kind of silence
that doesn't ask for anything
but to be felt.

Stay, not like a storm,
not like a fleeting dream,
but like the moon—
constant, gentle,
pulling me closer
without ever needing to speak.

Grand Delusion Of You

Ah, darling, love yourself—
Who else will do it with such blind devotion?
Stand before the mirror like a tragic masterpiece,
Smirk, sigh, twirl—yes, twirl—
You're the main character, after all.

Romanticize your own misery,
Wear heartbreak like designer couture,
Sip your morning tea as if it's laced with divine epiphanies,
And pretend the universe conspires solely for your
amusement.
(Spoiler: It doesn't, but let's not ruin the fantasy.)

Spin your flaws into poetry,
Call your stubbornness "willpower,"
Your chaos "artistry,"
Your bad decisions?
Ah, those are just "plot twists."

Love yourself so recklessly
That even narcissists take notes.
Stand in the storm and whisper,
"Yes, this is aesthetic."
Then trip over your own dramatic monologue,
Because irony is inescapable.

And when they ask, "Are you okay?"
Laugh like the protagonist of a French novel,
Gaze wistfully at the horizon,
And say,
"I was born for this tragedy."

But you weren't.
And that's the joke.

A Dream Of A Faceless Love

In twilight's veil, where shadows merge,
A faceless girl begins to surge,
Her touch is cold, yet strangely near,
A ghostly warmth, both dark and clear.

Her laughter echoes, distant, frail,
A haunting melody, soft and pale,
Each kiss a chill, both deep and sweet,
A promise in the night's deceit.

As dawn breaks through the shadowed seam,
You wake from this haunting dream,
The faceless love, with eerie charm,
Leaves an imprint, cold yet warm.

Though she's a phantom, lost in night,
Her essence lingers, soft and bright,
In dreams she dwells, where shadows play,
A love that guides you through the gray.

Always, Never

Always the angel, never the god,
Always the path, never the trod.
Always the whisper, never the cheer,
Always the shadow, never the clear.
Always the healer, never the healed,
Always the wound that has never yield.
Always the giver, never the gain,
Always the bearer of silent pain.
Always the poet, never the rhythm,
Always the endless wait for time.
Always the hope, never the day,
Always the dreams that slip away.
Always the strength, never the rest,
Always the weight over my chest.
Always the light, never the gleam,
Always the wish, never the dream.
Always the lover, never the love,
Always the story left untold.
Always the tears I cannot hide,
It at end, it is me.

An Apology To Myself

I'm sorry for the nights I cried alone
For the times I felt so far from home
For the days I let the darkness win
And silenced the voice deep within.
Forgive me for the dreams I let die
For the moments I didn't even try
For the love I pushed away in fear
And the times I couldn't see clear.
I'm sorry self for all the pain
I'm sorry for the harsh words I said to myself
Echoing in my head, for the times I couldn't
Believe in me and couldn't see what others saw...

Apocalypse

When the sky turned its final shade,
And the earth beneath us swayed,
In the silence of the end,
Echoes of the past ascend.

Cities crumbled into dust,
Dreams and hopes began to rust,
The stars blinked out, one by one,
As shadows swallowed the sun.

From the ashes, whispers rose,
Of forgotten tales and hidden woes,
A chorus of the world's last song,
Played by ghosts of what went wrong.

The oceans roared with ancient might,
Clashing waves against the night,
Mountains wept their stony tears,
For the end had drawn near.

As the final breath of day was drawn,
And the echoes of the world were gone,
A new dawn whispered, soft and keen,
In the ruins, a glimpse of what could be seen.

For in the dark of apocalypse's grace,
Where endings fade and shadows race,
The seeds of a new world took their stand,
In the fertile ashes of the land.

Autumn's Kiss

In shades of brown and golden light
Your presence turns the world to right.
Your laughter, like the autumn leaves
Rustling soft, it never expires.
In every moment that you're near
My heart whispers what you can't hear.
So tell me, could we be
More than glances, you and me?
Will you take this chance, my dear?
To hold our love forever near.
Will you walk this path with me?
And make our love an endless sea.
When you dream, do you realize I'm near?
Do you know how much I love you, my dear?

Bound By Fear

In the quiet of the night, it comes,
A heavy weight, a drum that drums,
Anxiety, with its tight embrace,
Takes our dreams and steals our space.

It whispers fears we can't escape,
A constant voice, a tangled tape,
We want to dance, to reach the sky,
But fear holds us back; we don't know why.

Plans we make are lost and fade,
In shadows dark, our hopes are stayed,
We sit and wait, afraid to try,
Bound by fears we can't deny.

Our hearts ache for a peaceful place,
Where worries vanish without a trace,
Yet every time we start to reach,
We find ourselves stuck on the beach.

But in the silence, there's a spark,
A tiny light that fights the dark,
Though fear holds us tight and near,
We hold on to the dreams we hold dear.

For even when anxiety binds,
We still have hopes and dreams to find,
And though it's hard, we'll find the way,
To break free and seize the day.

Curse Of Being Shy

I stand in shadows, always so shy
Letting moments pass me by
Words unsaid, locked in my chest
The fear of speaking never let me rest

I see you smile, but I look away
Hiding the thoughts I long to say
My silence, a prison I built so high
Now I'm left to wonder why

Regret fills the spaces where courage should be
What could have been, now I'll never see
Now it kills me, day by day
The chance I lost, the words that I didn't say

Shyness, my curse, my silent fear
Now I'm drowning in the night
It's simple, but it's true and clear
How I lost my words that you'd never hear...

Distant Hearts

53

We used to share our dreams and fears
In laughter, joy, and sometimes tears
But now a distance, wide and vast
Keeping us apart, our friendship past.
Hurdles stand in every way
People's words lead us astray
A bond once strong, now stretched so thin,
A silent ache deep within.
I miss the days, the talks we had, the moments good
The moments had, yet fate has placed us apart
With unseen walls of people closing our eyes around each
heart.
Not strangers, no, we know us too well,
The stories only we can tell.
But life has drawn a line so clear
Keeping you there and me here.

Echoes Of Unsaid Words

In the quiet corners of my mind
Unsaid words I always find
They linger there, a silent plea
Whispers of what we couldn't be.

Now those words they softly call
From the shadows through the hall
Reminding me of what's been missed
A silent story, a ghostly kiss.

If only I had found the voice
To speak the words, to make the choice
To say the things my heart held tight
To turn the wrong into right.

Moments passed, and chances lost
In the silence, I count the cost
A word of love, a tear unshed
Echoes of what went unsaid.

Endless Gratitude

In your eyes, I find my light
Guiding me through the darkest night
Your love, a shelter from the storm
In your embrace, I feel so warm.

When I was lost, you found the way
With gentle words you'd always say
"I'd be your guiding star" and
Now I see how right you are.

The sacrifices, all the care,
The countless ways you both are there
Your love a gift I can't repay
But in my heart, you'll always stay.

So thank you, Mom and Dad, so dear
For all you've done to bring near
Your love has shaped the person I am
Forever grateful, your loving lamb.

Fell First, Fell Hard

I saw you there; my heart did race
In a crowded room, I found my place
I fell first; I fell hard
Love hit me like a shooting star.

Your smile, a beacon, drew me in
A feeling strong, beneath my skin
I fell first; I fell deep
In dreams of you, my heart to keep.

But time passed by; you didn't see
The love I felt, the depth of me
I fell first; I fell alone
A silent wish, a love unknown

Yet here I stand, my heart still made of you
With love for you that can't be sold
I fell first, and still I'm falling hard
But in the end, you were my dream and someone else's reality.

First Of Poetry

there was a light far out there
striking my eyes, waiting for me to reach there
i'd stay there watching
wondering if fate ever had us
or a passerby ...found relative
are you the one i'd think forever
or a memory tryna delete, wishing i never met ya
oh, the poetic mind of me
turning a stranger into a poem
never mind, cause i've always been the poet
but never the poem
i stood there wasting my time
looking at you the way you'll never look at mine
my rivers flowed in you, but you let down the dam
but it had to flow somehow,
then why not let it shed down my eyes
not tears, just to make my vision bright
making it clear we are parallel lines
can we be adjacent, maybe once in a lifetime?

I Pretend I Don't Care

I pretend I don't care
Wear a mask every day; hide the tears, the fears, in shadows
they stay
With a smile so bright, no one sees the pain, a heart breaking
Softly like a quiet rain
In laughter, I cover the sorrow inside
The deep, aching void that I try to hide
No one suspects; no one can see
The battle within, a silent plea
I pretend I don't care
But inside, I'm torn
A soul that's been weathered, tattered, and worn
Yet I carry on, through each silent tear
Hoping someday, someone will hear

If The World Was Ending

If the world was ending what'd you do
Come and say something to me or forget me?
I doubt you knew what you meant to me
Cause maybe you thought of me as a normal lady attracted to
your external beauty
But what I desired was to drown inside that beauty of yours
But we never got to know each other, but when you come
close, I just tremble
I don't know what it all means, cause I have fallen for you
I read you through those drunk eyes of yours, but little did
you do anything,
Couldn't you give a flicker of a smile or a little hi, that
attitude darling

In the Glow of Twilight

In twilight's soft and gentle glow,
We met where only moonlight knows,
Your smile was like a warm embrace,
A fleeting touch, a tender grace.

The night was still, the stars aligned,
A whispered moment, yours and mine,
In the quiet, hearts took flight,
Underneath the silver light.

As dawn approached and dreams withdrew,
The night's enchantment lingered true,
A fleeting spark, a timeless grace,
In memories of that moonlit place.

Just The Way You Are, My Love

Your short hair frames your face so fine
In every strand, I see you shine
But know my love goes far beyond
Appearance changes, still I'm fond

Whether you grow your hair so long
Or keep it short, my love is strong
It's not the outside I adore
It's who you are really, your inner core

Your smile, your laugh, the way you care
These are the things that keep me there
No change in style could sway my heart
For we're connected, soul and part

My love for you like endless ways
Unchanged by trends or passing days
In every form, through every phrase
I'll love you always, all your days

So understand, my dearest mate
My love for you will never bend
In every look, in every way
My heart is yours, come what may

Lost in Shadows

In the silence of my room,
I feel the weight of empty gloom,
A map with no path to follow,
A heart that's heavy and hollow.

The days blend into endless gray,
With no clear start, no clear way,
I wander through a foggy night,
Searching for a distant light.

The echoes of my own regret
Are all that I can hear or get,
I reach for dreams that slip away,
And hope that fades with each new day.

Each step feels heavy, out of place,
In a world that's lost its grace,
I'm drifting through a sea of doubt,
With no direction, no way out.

The stars above seem cold and far,
Their light can't heal the unseen scar,
I stand alone, with no clear goal,
A ship adrift, a lost soul.

In the mirror, a stranger's face,
A shadow of a once-known place,
I search for peace; I search for more,
But find only a locked door.

I wish for signs, for guiding hands,
To lead me through these barren lands,
But in this dark and endless fight,
I'm lost and cannot find the light.

Love Of Sun And Moon

In ancient skies, where legend stays,
Lived sun and moon, both night and day.
He, the sun, with golden light,
She, the moon, with silver bright
The sun would rise so strong and bold
The moon would wait with hearts of gray
They'd meet at dawn, a tender kiss
This love a secret, sweet and bliss
As day turned night, and night turned day
Their hearts would ache, their love would sway
In twilight's glow, they'd touch then part
A timeless glow, a lover's art
In skies above, their tale is told
A love that aches, yet never grows old
For though they're apart, their love stays true
In every sunset, every hue
The sun and moon, forever near
Their love eternal, crystal clear
Their hearts forever intertwined
In the heavens, love defined

My Blood Is Not Mine

In shadows deep, where secrets lie
Our fate intertwined; we cannot deny
Your touch, your kiss a haunting sign
This blood that binds us is not mine
Whispers of the night we share
A love that's dark, beyond compare
Your heart, your soul, forever mine
Yet this blood runs in different line
Yet in this dark, romantic dance
We take our chance, a fleeting glance
Through shadows cast, in love's design
I vow to love you, cause this blood runs in you

Never Enough

In a world so vast, I stand alone
Good but not the best, never fully grown
Pretty but not the prettiest, in every crowd
A quiet soul, never too loud

Each smile I give, each tear I hide
A silent storm I carry inside
In a world that wants the best, the bright
I'm a flicker in the night

Good but not great; it's a bitter cap
A constant feeling of not being enough
I try so hard, give all my might
But somehow, it's never quite right

Pretty Shapes

In school hallways, whispers fly
Cruel words thrown without a why
They laugh and joke; it's all in fun
But the damage done can't be undone

They point and stare, a constant tease
Making comments with such an ease
They never see the pain inside
The tears we cry, the hurt we hide

We carry these wounds, day by day
Hoping one day the pain will sway
But the memories, they linger still
Every whisper, a bitter pill

Body shaming, a casual game
Leaves us feeling so much shame
Scars that cut deep into our soul
Leaving wounds that take the troll

We stand in front of mirrors, hating what we see
Wishing to be someone else, to be free
From the judgment, the endless taunts
The haunting words that forever haunt

Teenagers mock; they call it fun
But they don't see the harm they've done
We hate ourselves, can't escape
Their words shape how we see our shape
Don't. Just don't.

Secret Glance

In crowded halls, our eyes collide
A moment frozen, hard to hide
Your glances linger just as mine
A secret shared, a hidden sign
I see you there across the room
Your presence dispels my every gloom
Daydreams paint our secret world
Where whispered words and smiles reside
I wonder if you feel it too
The silent dance between us two.

Silent Scars

I don't talk much; words feel so rare
For every whisper, there's a wound left bare
Their voices cut, like knives they sting
Each word a lash, each phrase a ring
In the quiet corners, I seek my peace
Bandages don't heal words' wounds
The pain inside forever tuned
They never see the tears I hide
Or know how much they've hurt my pride
I don't talk because it hurts too much
The weight of words, the slightness touch
I hold my silence, my fortress strong
A shield against the cruel and wrong
Their words, they ripple through my mind
Leaving wounds, invisible but unkind
They say I'm shy; they say I'm weak
But they don't know the pain I seek
In every joke, in every sneer
Lies the reason I disappeared
They never realize the damage done
How their words have killed someone
So I stay quiet, my words restrained
To protect myself from being pained
For in the words, darkness lies,
That brings the tears and silent cries

The Celestial Cord

Beneath the moon's soft silver gaze,
Where constellations softly blaze,
A cord of fate is gently spun,
Binding hearts till night is done.

Two souls, adrift on cosmic seas,
Are drawn together by the breeze.
Though oceans vast and mountains high
May stretch between them, skies won't lie.

This thread, though hidden from the eye,
Is stitched with stars that never die.
Through dreams and whispers, hopes will guide,
As love's sweet song draws close beside.

In moments when the world seems cold,
And stories of the heart are told,
Know that the cord will pull you near,
A love eternal, crystal clear.

So when you seek your lover's face,
Look up to heaven, find your place,
For in the vast and endless blue,
The celestial cord will lead to you.

The Mind Game

In the dark where thoughts collide,
Shadows twist and secrets hide,
The mind's a maze of fear and gloom,
A twisted, cold, and silent room.

Whispers crawl beneath the skin,
Darkness waits, and fears begin,
Every thought a ghostly trace,
Every corner hides a face.

In the quiet, shadows creep,
In the silence, secrets sleep,
Thoughts unravel, dark and deep,
In the depths where shadows weep.

Heartbeats race in hidden dread,
Whispers dance around your head,
In this dark, suspenseful place,
The mind's a maze you can't escape.

The Weight Of What Could Be

You stood within reach for me to hold,
Yet I built walls with my silence.
A fortress of doubt, I built
Brick by brick,
Each one felt like a word I swallowed whole;
Now I'm left choking deep.

I saw the silent flicker in your eyes,
Questions waiting to be answered,
But I feared the question.
I feared the size of my voice
Straining the fragile string between us.
I let the moment pass,
Watched it dissolve like smoke in paradise.

We drifted—
Not from distance, but from pride,
A chasm carved by misunderstandings
We were too stubborn to bridge.
What was it we were so afraid of?
The truth,
Or the vulnerability it demanded?

Now, in this empty space,
I sift through the ashes of almost.
Laughter that could have been,
Touches that never came,
Lives we might have lived
If only I'd dared to step forward.

You were a universe,
And I chose to orbit in silence,
Content to watch your light from afar.
But stars don't wait,
and neither did you.

Regret is a slow poison,
And I drink it daily,
Tasting every moment
I let slip through my trembling hands.
I wonder if you remember
The things we never said—
The lives we could have woven
If courage had come sooner.

In the end, I lost you
Not to time,
Not to fate,
But to my own fear.
And I walk this hollow path alone,
Haunted by the weight
of what wasn't.

Till Death Do Us Part

Till death do us part, our love remains true
In the quietest moment, I'm thinking of you
Through joys and sorrows
We've come so far; together we shine
With every heartbeat, our promises we keep
In walking hours and in dreams deep
No storm can break what we have sworn
A love eternal, ever reborn
Till death do us part, my soul's embrace
In every lifetime, in every place
Our heaths are only bound by fate
Together forever, love never abates

Torn Pages From An Old Book

In an old diary, worn and torn
Are pages of friendship, now forlorn
Each word a memory, each line a scar
A story of us from days so far

Your laughter is in the faded ink
Now like stars that slowly sink
I trace my words with shaky hands
Remembering dreams and old plans

We were best friends, or so it seemed
But time broke apart our dreams
Promises made when we were young
Now feels like shadows sad song sung

I wonder if you think of me
When you see stars or hear the thundering
Do our laughs still haunt your mind?
Do the memories of us still unwind?

These old pages hold my heart
From a time we didn't part
They remind me of a bond so pure
Of a friendship I thought would forever endure

Now I'm here alone with these lines
Missing you deeply, across the times
In this diary, where memories sleep
I find my sorrow and quietly weep

True Beauty

95

You say you're not perfect; you hide your face
Worried about looks, feeling out of place
But if only you could see what I can see
You'd know how truly beautiful you can be

Your short hair frames a face so bright
A smile that shines a pure delight
Each glance you give, a world unfolds
A beauty far beyond what mirror holds

You are more than what you lack
A pretty soul, no need to hold back
If you could see yourself through my eyes
You'd understand, you're a treasure in disguise

Undesired Obsession

In the dead of night, I lie awake,
Haunted by a love I can't partake,
A shadowed dream I can't embrace,
A ghost that haunts a hollow space.

Your name's a whisper in my mind,
A fleeting touch I'll never find,
I chase your silhouette in vain,
Lost in the echo of my pain.

Your laughter's a distant song,
In a world where I don't belong,
I reach for you through endless night,
But find only the cold moonlight.

Every thought, a twisted chain,
Binding me to endless pain,
A love that's never meant to be,
A prison built inside of me.

In the darkness, I still yearn,
For a flame that will not burn,
A cruel obsession, sharp and deep,
A love I mourn while I still weep.

Unspoken Regret

I tried so hard to make you proud
To hear your praise, to stand out loud
But in my efforts, I lost my way
And now I stand in dismay
Your dreams for me, I couldn't fulfill
Each missed step, a bitter pill
Your hopes and wishes, high and bright
Now seem so distant, out of sight
I see the sadness in your eyes
A quiet tear that never dries
I wanted to be your shining star
But here I've fallen apart
Your words of love, though still they come
Feel like a weight I can't hold no more
I wish I could turn back the time
To find a way to make you proud
So forgive me, for your dreams I broke
For every tear and word unspoken
I tried so hard, but lost the fight
In the shadows of your guiding star.

Weight Of Tears

A single tear falls
Silent and slow
A world of heartache flows in its gentle streams
It holds the weight of those unsaid, hidden deep words
Of dreams shattered and love that hurts.
Each drop a story unforgotten, each a pain
Silent witnesses to the heart's refrain.
In its deep, a soul's deep cry
A whisper of sorrow, an unsaid, muted goodbye
For tears are not weaknesses, but are a silent art,
A mirror reflecting the depths of someone's heart.

* 9 7 8 9 3 6 9 5 3 7 3 4 1 *